STATES OF MATTER
Liquids

by Jim Mezzanotte

Reading consultant: Susan Nations, M.Ed., author/literacy coach/
consultant in literacy development
Science and curriculum consultant: Debra Voege, M.A., science
and math curriculum resource teacher

Please visit our web site at: www.garethstevens.com
For a free color catalog describing Weekly Reader® Early Learning Library's list
of high-quality books, call 1-877-445-5824 (USA) or 1-800-387-3178 (Canada).
Weekly Reader® Early Learning Library's fax: (414) 336-0164.

Library of Congress Cataloging-in-Publication Data

Mezzanotte, Jim.
  Liquids / by Jim Mezzanotte.
    p. cm. — (States of matter)
  Includes bibliographical references and index.
  ISBN-10: 0-8368-6799-8 — ISBN-13: 978-0-8368-6799-2 (lib. bdg.)
  ISBN-10: 0-8368-6804-8 — ISBN-13: 978-0-8368-6804-3 (softcover)
  1. Liquids—Juvenile literature. I. Title. II. Series.
  QC145.24.R93   2006
  530.4'2—dc22   2006012395

This edition first published in 2007 by
Weekly Reader® Early Learning Library
A Member of the WRC Media Family of Companies
330 West Olive Street, Suite 100
Milwaukee, WI 53212 USA

Copyright © 2007 by Weekly Reader® Early Learning Library

Editor: Gini Holland
Art direction: Tammy West
Cover design and page layout: Charlie Dahl
Picture research: Diane Laska-Swanke

Picture credits: Cover, title, © Royalty-Free/CORBIS; p. 5 NASA Goddard Space Flight Center;
pp. 7, 15, 16, 17 Melissa Valuch/© Weekly Reader Early Learning Library; pp. 8, 19 © Diane
Laska-Swanke; p. 9 © Michael Newman/PhotoEdit; p. 11 © Barbara Stitzer/PhotoEdit; p. 12
© Scientifica/Visuals Unlimited; pp. 13, 18 © David Young-Wolff/PhotoEdit; p. 20 © Kim
Fennema/Visuals Unlimited; p. 21 © Gregg Otto/Visuals Unlimited

Printed in the United States of America

1 2 3 4 5 6 7 8 9 10 09 08 07 06

Table of Contents

Cover and title page: Water is the most common — and best-known — liquid on earth.

Chapter One

A Liquid World

Liquids are a form of matter. Do you know what matter is? It is all around you. It is anything that takes up space and has **weight**.

Oceans and mountains are matter. The air we breathe is matter, too. Plants and animals are matter. People are, too. Almost everything in the universe is matter.

Matter can be in different forms, or states. It can be a **solid** or a **gas**. It can also be a liquid. Solids hold their own shape. Liquids do not. They take the shape of what holds them. You can pour a liquid. It stays together as it moves, or flows.

Liquids are everywhere. A liquid covers most of Earth. It is called water! Milk is a liquid. Orange juice is a liquid. Paint is a liquid, too. What liquids can you find?

In this photograph, you can see Earth's blue oceans. Water covers most of our planet.

Chapter Two

Properties of Liquids

There are many kinds of liquids. How can we describe them? The ways we describe them are called **properties**.

Volume is the amount of a liquid. It is the space a liquid takes up in a container. At the store, you could buy milk. How much do you want? You could buy 1 quart or 1 liter. A family might buy 1 gallon or 4 liters.

A liquid can change shape. But even if it does, its volume stays the same.

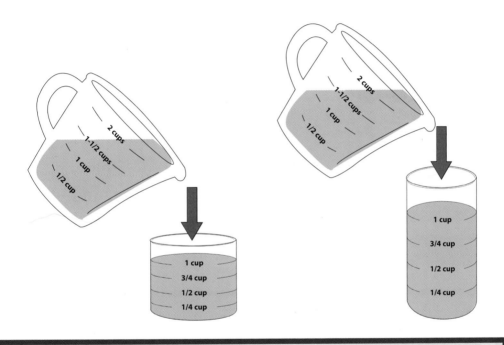

TRY THIS: Pour some water into a short, wide glass. Now, pour the same amount into a tall, skinny glass. The volume is the same in both glasses.

Liquids have weight. First, weigh an empty glass. Then, weigh the glass filled with water. Subtract the weight of the glass. You have the water's weight.

A liquid has a certain **density,** too. Two liquids can fill up spaces that are the same size. But one can weigh more. It is denser. In its space, it has more **molecules**. They are the tiny pieces that make up all matter.

TRY THIS: Pour water into one glass. Pour cooking oil into another glass. Make sure the amounts are the same. Now, weigh both liquids. They each have the same volume. But the water is heavier. It has a higher density.

Some liquids flow quickly. They are not very thick. Others, such as syrup, flow slowly. They are thick.

Oils are a certain kind of liquid. They are smooth and slippery. They are hard to wipe away.

Maple syrup is a thick liquid. It pours out very slowly.

Chapter Three

Hot and Cold

In the cold, a pond may turn into ice. The water turns into a solid. Water turns into a solid at a certain temperature. It is called the **freezing point**. Different liquids have different freezing points.

What happens if it gets warm? The pond melts. The ice turns into a liquid again.

Heat makes many solids turn into liquids. Wax and chocolate turn into liquids when they get warm. They turn back into solids when they get cold again.

These children are skating on a hard solid called ice. Water changes when it gets very cold. It turns from a liquid into a solid.

After a while, this puddle will disappear. It will turn into a gas. The gas rises up in the air.

Heat can turn a liquid into a gas. What happens to puddles after the rain stops? They seem to disappear. The Sun warms them. The water **evaporates**. It slowly turns into a gas called water vapor.

Have you ever seen water boil? As the water gets hot, bubbles form. Inside these bubbles, water has turned into gas. The bubbles rise to the surface. They "pop." The gas goes into the air.

Water boils at a certain temperature. It is called the **boiling point**. Different liquids have different boiling points.

This water is boiling. Some of it has turned into gas. The gas is in the bubbles.

Water evaporates from oceans. It evaporates from lakes and rivers, too. The water vapor goes into the air as a gas.

High up where the air is colder, the water vapor turns back into liquid. It forms clouds. Rain or snow falls from the clouds.

The water seeps into the ground. It goes back into the oceans, lakes, and rivers. This water **cycle** happens again and again.

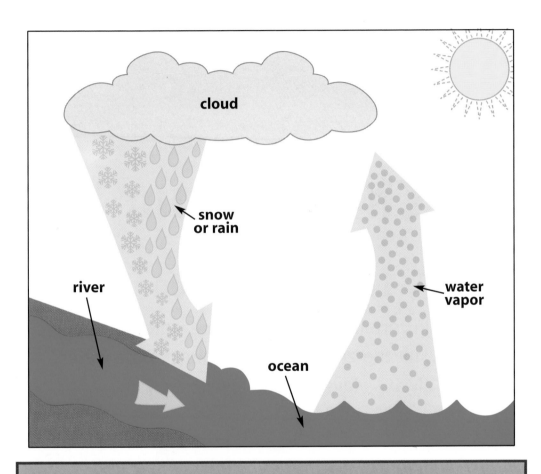

Earth's water cycle never stops. During part of the cycle, water turns from a liquid into a gas. Then it turns back into a liquid, forming clouds.

Chapter Four

Liquids in Action

Liquids act in certain ways. Pour some water into a glass. Now, tilt the glass. What happens to the water? Its surface always stays flat and level.

You can tilt a glass of water. But the water's surface stays level.

A liquid cannot be squashed to fit a smaller space. Imagine you have a glass full of water. You place a wooden block in it. There is not enough room for the block and the water. The water cannot be squashed. Some of it spills out of the glass. The block takes up a certain space. The water that spills would fill this space exactly.

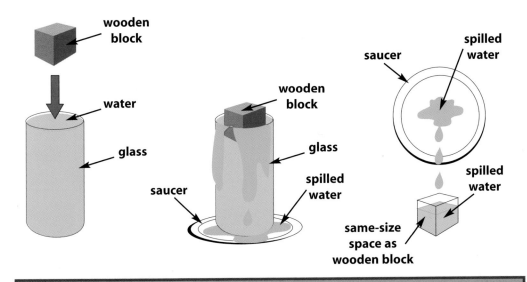

A block goes into a full water glass. Some water spills out. A saucer holds the spilled water. This water would fill the same space as the block.

Liquids can mix together. Many mix with water. Look around your home. Can you find liquids with water in them? How about shampoo? Liquids can mix with solids. Water and dirt can mix to make mud. They can mix with gases, too.

Chocolate syrup and milk are liquids. You can mix them together to make chocolate milk.

18

Paints are liquids. You can mix paints to make different colors.

Some liquids do not mix together. Water and oil, for example, do not mix. Have you ever seen pictures of an oil spill in the ocean? The oil floats on the surface. But it does not mix with the water.

This bottle holds oil and vinegar. They are not mixed together. The oil floats on top. It is lighter than vinegar.

We could not live
without water and
other liquids. They
are an important
part of our world!

Water is an important
liquid. We could not
live without it!

Glossary

boiling points — the high temperatures a liquid must reach to boil, turning into a gas

cycle — things happening again and again, in the same order

density — the mass of something when it has a particular volume Density measures how many molecules of something are in a certain space

evaporate — turn from a liquid to a gas

freezing point — the low temperature a liquid must reach to turn into a solid

gas — a form of matter. A gas cannot hold its own shape It expands to fill whatever is holding it, and it is not usually visible

molecules — tiny pieces of matter. A molecule is two or more atoms joined together. Atoms are the building blocks of all matter

properties — ways of describing something. Volume, mass, and density are all properties of a liquid

solid — a form of matter. A solid can hold its own shape. This shape can be changed, but a solid will not change shape on its own

volume — the space a liquid takes up in a container, which is the amount of the liquid

weight — measuring the force of gravity on an object

For More Information

Books

Everyday Physical Science Experiments with Liquids. Science
  Surprises (series). Amy French Merrill. (Powerkids Press)

Solids, Liquids, and Gases. Rookie Read-About Science (series).
  Ginger Garrett. (Children's Press)

Water Cycle. Nature's Patterns (series). Monica Hughes. (Millbrook)

Web Sites

Science Clips: Solids and Liquids

www.bbc.co.uk/schools/scienceclips/ages/8_9/solid_liquids.shtml
This interactive site has many fun ways to learn about solids and
liquids, for children of different ages.

Solids and Liquids

www.fossweb.com/modulesK-2/SolidsandLiquids
At this site, you can learn about how matter changes form.

Water

www.nyu.edu/pages/mathmol/textbook/3gradecover.html
Visit this site to learn about water as a liquid, solid, and gas.

Publisher's note to educators and parents: Our editors have carefully reviewed these Web
sites to ensure that they are suitable for children. Many Web sites change frequently, however,
and we cannot guarantee that a site's future contents will continue to meet our high standards
of quality and educational value. Be advised that children should be closely supervised
whenever they access the Internet.

Index

About the Author

Jim Mezzanotte has written many books for children. He lives in Milwaukee with his wife and two sons.